PEACE, RHODODENDRON

PEACE, RHODODENDRON

POETRY

ELIZABETH LEVERTON

Copyright © 2023 by Elizabeth Leverton

All rights reserved.

No part of this book may be reproduced in any form or by any electronic or mechanical means, including information storage and retrieval systems, without written permission from the author, except for the use of brief quotations in a book review.

ISBN: 978-1-946052-47-6 (PRINT)

Editing, Interior and Cover Design by James D. McCallister/Mind Harvest Press
www.jamesdmccallister.com

Contents

December	1
The Thrill of a Cubist Thought	3
Theoretical Connection	5
The Road That Will Lead Me Home	7
Space Face On The Moon	9
The Rose	11
For Hart Crane	13
Last Glimpse	15
When Names Become Lost	17
Chasing Spirits	19
Ancient Eyes	21
In Search of Blue	23
Kiss Me Goodbye Again	25
The Idea Maker	27
I Want To Know 8 Minutes Ago	31
God Came to Me	33
Ashes	35
There Will Be Less in a Moment	37
Isle Awhile	39
Ben Franklin Works 3rd Shift	41
I Long To See You Awakening	43
Honeycomb	45
My Peace On This Thanksgiving	47
What Love Is	51
Cool Night Blue	53
Winter	55
You, Mr. Whitman	57
Our Tree	59
Eggshells	61
Peace, Rhododendron	63
If We Can Keep It	65
We Called You Chief	67
Exhausting All Media	69
Black Slush on the Roadside	73
Daybreak	75
Here	77

The Key of Light	79
We'll Feed the Animals	81
Acknowledgments	89
About the Author	93

for

*those
who find some
reassurance
here*

Ce sont les rêves.

December

Dr. Dude left me rocking in the easy chair
while performing psychotherapy
for the kids at WFU, and once I worked
up a dollar appetite he sent Bernardin
to buy me a sandwich.

We ended up in a small town where the
hyenas block the roads, me, up in a tree
holding onto branches while he stood below,
trying to shake me down. Someone was
following me, almost dreamlike—then
we reached a cabin-full who were planning
to sing some tribal songs.

It was the Grateful Dead (they didn't
remember me, but I fixed coffee anyway,
forgetting my wits and subsiding to the slow,
rocking *baht bah baht bah*, making two cups
instead of thirty, and I spilled one trying to
make it down the stairs where I bumped into
a young girl who was obviously lying
about her past yet seemingly truthful
in her knowledge and remembrance
of American history.

For example, she said, "Millard Fillmore was
the 13th President," and I agreed, glad to see
someone remembering *something*—
isn't that what language is for?)

My charge-card statement came with a
$24,000 credit for this poem, and I paid
this kid on a moped $70 to bring me home.

The Thrill of a Cubist Thought

I.

Once again I teeter at the edge.
Mapping tree bark, I study the river.
These are not the rapids of a friendly,
adventurous day; their roaring sound
sings the flat notes of my disease and at once I
    wish the water would make me lost.

My companions—
they look like shadows now—
stand on the pebbles of the shore,
waiting for my great change.
My tears are ice-cold
and they prick my face like pin-tips.

II:

Sometimes, she tells me,
it is enough just to put on the armor.
Take it off, and do it again.
Sometimes it is all we can do.

I drag out the armor.
I put it on.
I will do it again and again.

There are those of us who will practice
for a lifetime.
I like to think of butter that is melting.

III.

But I get this weird feeling.
As my foot kicks ellipses of sand into
the river below, I unsteadily turn
and return to the woods.

I know I could answer the great question
if a clue would present itself.

But life's a test I'm trying to write,
without preparation—or foresight.
My attempts at wry choices embarrass me.
My fill-in-the-blanks skirt
the pathway of sense
like bits of crumbs,
suited only for birds.
(I settle on the open-ended questions that will
    eddy us into eternity.)

IV.

If I give you these questions,
I will have to, I'll listen as your answers
depart from me. I need you, though—
the nighttime always blows me away.
Tonight I whistle while drawing stars—

       with a super-sharp pencil...

               and it's 4 o'clock.

Theoretical Connection

I been knocking
on wood.
I been
whispering
to myself: this is no ordinary
promise,

        this connection,

      simon-pure,

bonafide,
genuine.

This love

        forever

This love

        walks alone

This love

has a string around its finger,

>   it remembers,
>   it unfolds
>   it transcends
>   any need

to walk alone,
but cheek

>   by jowl; side by side

>   we knock on wood.

The Road That Will Lead Me Home

If I were asked to run these rapids,
I wouldn't; I'd take the road around and walk
'til dehydration set in, and I wouldn't even ask
for water, not until I was looking
at the wild-eyed face of death.

Maybe once she had eased me down,
and when I'd found a place to lie,
like face down on a circle of moss
that could have been laid by a fairy host,
reclining knee-deep in ethereal bubbles,
or settled like a bee on honeycomb—

Maybe then, perhaps, I'd say,
Just one more thing, Death.
—Give me a glass of water
higher than the rapids
and colder than Chicago rain.
Give me then just a thimbleful more,
namely, in my grandmother's
commemorative Jimmy Carter thimble
filled to its
rim,

and into my heart, Death, stitch freedom,
and put me on the backs of those I'll leave
behind, those braver than I, and stronger—
for one last ride.

Let me lead them down this river of disaster
without a wince;
let me reanimate love in all of her calm;
let you choke on your expectations,
Death,

as we ride those summer-stormy waves—

& I
am not
afraid.

Space Face On The Moon

I.

I welcome the thought of you,
and urge you into my space.

I cannot distinguish your face;
do not see the subtle mechanics
of your smile.

Your laugh sounds like a sister's,
but I do not see your eyes
as they crinkle in delight.

I look up at the ceiling,
out the window at the dark night.

"No no no," says my mind. Tic toc, tic toc:
"No no no." It is trying to erase logic.

I need you even more now that you are gone.
You would explain my loss to me,
this feeling of permanent depth.
"No no no." "No no no."

II.

I try to create thunder in my ears,
but quiet rain keeps falling down.

I drag up an empty chair
to pretend that you are here.

I try to sing, but I can't breathe.

Do you soar? Are you free?
Are you flying overhead?

I long for signs— but what? and where?
The grass — the trees — the sky — the air.

The moon is coming round again:
The stars, the sun, the sun, the sky,
the sky, the sun, the moon, the stars—

Suddenly—Your laugh again:
You await me everywhere.

The Rose

It is not a circle
nor other
but almost a triangle.

It rains and
we put our noses to the
indescribable

smell of the rose.
We find sunlight there.
Its color is not red

and not pink or orange,
not like the fading light,
but close.

What we smell of its flesh
is not a smell at all,
but a memory.

What we touch
is not a vision of what was
but of who we are

on mornings
when we rise, and for no reason,
feel joy.

For Hart Crane

The sky of the pieces of life embedded in the
    imaginary, in happiness and fortitude is
    wrapping the arms of inconsistency with
    ruby-red ribbon and gold.

Faces.

There are questions in the minds of the young as
    they trample and frolic and stand

kissing the winter air while playing icicle-songs
    with tree branches held in wet, frozen hands.

They are strong and not yet forceful—
they have not stumbled yet on what controls
    them.

There are trees here
but there is some evil in the world.

It chases us and our shortcomings,
block after block.

You, elusive Proteus, were our gentle Van Gogh,
    and wrote your life's homage to love.

Patience is weird. It is invisible and then it
    altogether disappears.

This, then, is the way of growing old:
grief, no grief, grief, no grief.

Life begins, at any rate,
without much.

Last Glimpse

of a 49¢ Orphan's Dream

I have heard the songs of sailors
whose ships were wrecked by night,
and the wooden-footed soldiers
who fought for what they felt was right.
I believe in things I cannot see —
I fly by night —
I see red flares.
I wave the flag of our young nation.
Its tears were wrought by iron-forged tools
in the hands of our original few, who have
asked only of me:
"What does freedom mean to you?"

In answer to those silent auctioneers
I offer this in selflessness:
I am a simple man
who has tried to understand
what I cannot comprehend,
and yet joyously strive to.
I have lived in the belly of Black Magic
    mountains,
seeking worth; seeking self; seeking love —
not loathing — simply, seeking peace.

I have walked at midnight
down each trembling path, burdened by fear,
longing to execute by example
the stuttering complacency
of those who are unwise.

I have taken fast rides
on slow trains,
longing to be decent,
hoping for heavenly rest,
wishing to remember those coming before me,
who strayed in seeming uselessness
in search
of water & sky —

following the moon and the stars.

When Names Become Lost

I.

In his eyes, life
In his eyes, a smile.
His quiet voice said, "See ya after awhile."
But I could not care for him, nor him for me;
We were both running wild,
passing as fish in the night
aboard the sea.

We were on a waiting list,
part of an unknown plan—
waiting for fate to turn us by its great hand.
When we had our photograph taken together
we smiled
but only on the inside.

II.

It was beyond limit,
beyond articulated observation,
why we met at this moment through
life's mediation.
He was a man, not a child and not old,
I was a wreck, dragged in off the broken road.

We lost nothing between us but names
when we parted,
illustrating our lack of connection
in a simple way.

We can add up the countless bills that we've paid,
ending up lost
as neither friends nor enemies,
like desert kites without their strings.

Once, tho—I remember,
how we cared
to linger there.

Chasing Spirits

I don't talk when I'm thinking of you,
when in my mind I'm twining with you,
like an ivy vine I climb with you,
jilted by time, space, and pining.

Castle wall, I saw you. You were so
proud, and 10-, 12-, 14 feet tall,
and in the sunshine you looked immaculate—
like the dance of dawn
between the sun and moon.

I imagine that everything I do is done by you,
that each thing I think, or stoop
to pick up off the street,
is a part of you,
and like a puzzle solved before a clue.

The solutions, I imagine, I borrow from you.
Memories flood in from another place,
and then I think I've seen your face:
your touch, the garden wall, an eagle flying.

Ancient Eyes

Standing by a window
I glimpsed the white-moth spirit of an ancestor.
He walked by me & around
this massive plot of land—
his haunt, his obsession.

I began to kick ivy
in search of the overgrown frog pond
we hear at night.

I creep around, I
look through windows while

"You must love what you do not know," he says—.

Is it likely to know the hearts of our dead?
I count the signs of my breathing.
I create memory:

His is the spirit of my days,
his words my tonic.
"You must love
what you do not love."

It is hard
to resolve anything with the living,
and unquestionably so with the dead.

In Search of Blue

I was sitting in a bus station surrounded
by Monks.
I was reading the funny papers.

You walked by me so reverently, so slowly,
and all of you made me feel like vapor in a cloud.
I reached out my hands,
touching the sleeves of your heavenly garb,
while on a suitcase a man placed a cross with his
    arms,
and one with his legs.

"Strike Anywhere," the matches said to me,
so I striked 'em in the bathroom on the bus.

I walked so heavy in Memphis
singing lonely-elephant-walking blues—
'til an angel walked me back to the nowhere from
    whence I had come,
such a long mile ago,
'til he told the driver I was mute—
"And she wants to get back on."

Alice's desperation
kept me walking lost ground

'Til I awakened at St. Mary's and knew
I'd been found.

Kiss Me Goodbye Again

I.

In my mind I saw you, like a wandering Ace,
You swam through water that
the cat knocked over and I swam too. I was
 looking for you.
Trapped in a world of mistreatment and lies
I beheld you as my angel.
You stood strong, and your words
touched me so deeply
it seemed that I could fly. You read me stories
and through the pain of seeing what I was not
came a slurring inability to see anything at all.
I, maniacal, felt
I had lost you because I had lost myself.
I reached for you to tell you that
the words I had written
were for your soul alone,
and in the belly of an ocean
I heard myself screaming quietly.

II.

Everyone wondered how I could look so different,
when even the two photographs of me,
frail with confusion and loss,
looked different from each other.
You and your friend sent colorful cards
that I cut into pieces and hung around the room.
I accepted flowers and performed delicate
surgeries on them, gardening in my room
at night when everyone else
was asleep. Across the hall she wrote to me,
"Fuck her- She is nobody to treat you like that. Do
    not worry or for that matter cry."
I held tightly to her acceptance of my *self*
and to your ditto marks, the
long talks over coffee, in a cryptic tongue
far away from here.

III.

In a crowd of people I spoke but could not see,
    and you, Doctor,
gave me sight by reminding me to listen. I heard
sounds that proved my childhood was over,
and colors that faced the colorblind with bleach—
all memories to me.

Your voice led me
to hear the dream of the muses,
and I still remember the sound,
of you pulling me up from the bottom,
wringing me out,
telling me softly, to fly—fly.

The Idea Maker

I saw the Ace of Spades walk in
with the Queen of Hearts
She was dressed just like the Eight of Diamonds.

I saw the baker snub the joker by
wearing a checkered suit—
Red, Black, White./ I saw an angel
drawing circles of magic on the floor.
Her shoes were on the wrong feet/
She had five sisters.

We braided a game out of stray cat hair and
her mother cast spells to make her forget;
I like to think she remembered.

I sat listening to a man who
talked like skipping stones,
Started every joke with the same line--
A man went into a bar/
A man went into a bar, right
On into secrets of International Importance.
He talked only to me, A man
went into a bar...

I lived with a girl who stole my clothes
and then washed everyone else's on my dime
    when I wasn't looking
She walked through any door like it was a Big
    Welcome Mat
Everyone thought she was crazy/I listened to her
    stories of men who lived
in garbage cans and
They were small men.

Somebody gave me a guitar
& I began to love reality.
He said he wanted to arrange a concert/He was
    looking for athletes/
I never played that thing very well—
So I gave it back to him for a T-shirt and he took
    the guitar— /& disappeared—

I knew a man
who was so old and so thin
he couldn't keep his pants up
He said
He had two hound dogs
I never met them
He said they were nice dogs.

I ate broccoli whenever I wanted
But I'd said I didn't like it
for exponential good reasons, and
I sat on the porch playing no-card-games-of-cards

        with my friend Jim

        Everyone was scared of him/

He was my strength.
But I never was too friendly with him, tho-
He a King
I a Jack

We watched the Ace of Spades
court the Queen of Hearts
over and over/again and again/ SAILING

                out on that porch

A man went
A man went into
A man went into a bar/ We were HIDING
from the heat
and smoking cigarettes/ Every Day /
We were there

Crossing our legs, uncrossing them,
clearing our throats,
expecting new World War in cahoots<
We were dreaming in a common tongue
and never laughing.

Have you ever been there/Where we've been/
Do you know what it's like to know so much
raging nonsense?

Do you know the convenience
of wearing OTHER PEOPLE'S CLOTHES?

I Want To Know 8 Minutes Ago

I was driving down the road
looking for the simple signs
of the life of the beach
that I remembered from my past,
the place
where the roadside quickly becomes
more of an island;
where broken shells lie skirting the asphalt
while the air becomes so rich
with the unmistakable smell of the sea.

I was young and in love once too, you see,
wanting to feel believed in:

When I undocked my boat one silent night,
what boatman was aware
how I had strayed to become wayward there,
and what indecencies and foolishness to which
I was wise
made my boat row on
while yet I capsized?

God Came to Me

I would have this recurring dream as a child,
that I was outside in the dark trying to get
home. A man would be walking the street,
as tall as my grandfather. He was trying to
give me a lighted candy cane.

When I entered psychotherapy as an adult,
the lighted candy cane became a burden of my
disorder, and that was that, the be-all and
end-all to twenty years of dreams about
little-me trying to get home in the dark.

Then one day I had another dream. It was
raining, and I ran out in the rain, pulled dead
plants and with their seeds planted again.
I placed a small branch of a flowering tree
deep within an old tree stump. In my dream,
the little tree grew,
and you were pleased and would say,
"she planted that tree right there,
the day she passed away."

Then I awakened, and tried to live up to my
only-the-good-die-young myth
misunderstanding.

One day, God came to me and said,
"Eleanor, dear, you are not the stuff that
myths are made of.
You must be—
without needing to be."
And God walked away. It was a cheerful day,

and later I went to the park
and looked at the funny people in the dark.

Ashes

Should I *tell the tale entire?*
Should I now recall the fire?

The overdose of life I took?
The memories I never shook?

I want to piece it all one day
to show how I respect the way

God made me be and think and feel—
then how He gave me ways to heal—

to gather up my fallen dreams,
and figure "it" from what it seems,

so I could one day hear you care,
and melt away my frantic scares.

There Will Be Less in a Moment

Stories stick to us like shadows
of our lives.
I remember a trail of stones,
or breadcrumbs—
a rhyming fall.

If I could forget the nights
that brought me to sea bottom,
I would say to you who *you* are, my love—
because somehow, beneath the cheerfulness,
I am melting.

My identifications, tho, if you can see it:
are just little crabapples, fallen from a tree
that is so very beautiful
as it leans in a weeping way outside the window
where the sun is beaming in
and the cats are sleeping.

People say that life
is short, but to others
it is very long,
especially
when beginning again—if all's lost.

The widening gyre
boggles my mind, drifting me off to that sea...
but firmly, I believe in peace.

(No one intends to write a tragedy,
and resilience is a great page-turner.
You catch nothing and
recast the net.)
A friend saves me from darkness again.

To me, to have begun again
is to become alive again:

You are the silver in my smile,
which keeping: keeps...
and keeps...
for a while.

Isle Awhile

After the weekend the beach is quiet
and the sound of the waves,
like a crowd,
is the only thing you hear.
Two girls lie facing the sand.
They have been down there for hours,
only standing occasionally to move their blanket,
and follow the sun.
The water dares to chase them slowly up the
    beach and there are
birds everywhere. Shadows on the beach
mime the grace of bird flight—still shadows,
sailing over the sands.
A young boy walks close to the water,
carrying a surfboard.
He passes the two girls, and turns,
passing them again.
When he turns again you laugh at his
    youthfulness,
as your eyes turn to an old man seemingly asleep
    by the pool.
His sunburn matches his red swimsuit, or blends,
    and he is wearing tennis shoes and white
    ankles
and sensing your gaze, he looks up at you.
His hat, a straw hat with two-inch ribbon

around it, sits on the chair beside him, and
when he stretches his arms above his head,
you, defying his obvious displeasure at being
watched from the 3rd floor, become fixed on
the whiteness of his underarms.
Red and white, this man is content.
He rolls over on his side.

Your eyes move back to the sand,
down the beach, skimming over
the twigs on a blanket.
A short man, leathered from the sun,
walks by the two girls with a metal detector,
seeking, seeking;
longing and enjoying
the tease of the beach.

Skimming over the white crests,
the green water,
sailing like birds
in the blue,
your eyes follow the waves out
to the line
that vaguely defines the water and sky.

How many times have you lingered here?

How many hours, grasping at eternity,
desiring so much more?

What have you then promised the horizon?

Ben Franklin Works 3rd Shift

I.

I like my late at night,
I like my coffee buzz
after dinner.
I like my *contemplative still*
in darkness, or by the light
of the midnight moon.
I like the quiet suggestion of TV
in the other room
that ensures these hours
aren't spent alone.
I like reading John Locke and I like drawing little
    stars
with sharp pencils, at 4 o'clock. I like rain
on the roof at 4:35.
To go to sleep by the quiet of 5:00.
This time of night, the going is still.

II.

With the window raised I hear a
train drag by in explicit detail.
My dog scratches decidedly
on the door.
The train doesn't click-clack
it raps its beat
like a snare, and sounds like it might fall
down the hill and into my kitchen sink.
Traffic signals are flashing
and streets echo with a likable stillness
as night places a last-minute call to morning.
Outside my window, the train tracks—
they are whistling now—call out
to this lithe hour.

I Long To See You Awakening

I.

Beneath these cotton candy aimless skies
I come upon a peacefulness in you
like that of the love of a father.

Men wander our bountiful lands
in search of our sons and daughters:

*We always remember the baseball
we didn't catch
The one fish we didn't throw back
The gifts we've accepted when
we could not give back.*

*We are prisoners of what is less
And we are surely better.*

*We are the believers of the Great Plan.
We break our bread because we share.*

II.

You have walked
briskly in dangerous times
carrying your dreams
in satchel-books of rhymes.

Some roads you knew took indecent turns,
leaving you thirsting in the burning sun.

I'm looking for our searching men,
for I have seen how souls get lost:
that a lost soul runs like a scared rabbit running,
that even the grizzly bear must keep vigil.

I long to show you that you have all night,
to reclaim your broken lives...

For twenty years I have walked you home.
I long to remind you: Your work now is done.

Honeycomb

Let me explain to you your colors.
You have no narcissistic gaze.
Yet you look at yourself in the mirror
and you look all in pieces.

So you are on a search, well,
that's not always a chore
but not always easy, either.
You could say you believe
you're on the right track—
getting close—
about to find your grail, meet your challenge,
leave your mark—
but then, maybe, you lean your head down,
saddened,
distrusting your sad self.
Blake's answer to the atheists was this:
"You throw sand against the wind
and the wind blows it back again."
An unknown author says he meant this:

You cannot outwit God.

What a marvelous idea.

And you, with your self-doubt,
you try your best to be best best in His eye.
You keep one ear toward Faith because you
know—
You get this feeling that God knows you:
& records your pages, your history.
& sees through your eyes, sees what you see.
& walks your footsteps, walking
where you walk.

You are spacious, and
You are a thumbprint.

"But," you tell me, you had no doubt in God.
I say when you doubted you you doubted
God, and you cannot
throw sand into the wind.

My Peace On This Thanksgiving

I.

The walls of the cafeteria seemed dusty.
The light from the windows seemed like
darkness, while I sat missing you.

Though I was only ten, you had been
gone most of my life and there was an
emptiness where you should have been
standing, Grandfather.
In my childish way I needed you.

I built a mansion in my mind. It was like
heaven, I suppose.
I thought if only we could all live together
in that one big house,
together forever, there would never be another
need for the great sadness I felt.

Nineteen years later it seems unusual to me
that I could have felt
so deeply a loss I couldn't possibly have
remembered. I was not even two
when you died.

My memories of you are memories of
someone else I have confused with you.

The voice I hear may be yours. It may be from
stories I have heard about you.

II.

When I became an adult I still searched for
some connection to you. I answered voices I
heard that sounded like yours.
I sat next to men dressed like you,
in fishing gear, baseball caps, wrinkled suits.

You found me once as I looked through that
slit in the sky.
You guarded my life, because I was careless
with it trying to get to you.
We played cards in my dreams and you taught
me new games.

When I walked I followed you. I found clues
to your existence.
I knew you were sending reassurance.
I never knew how to answer,
and tell you how un-reassuring the presence
of your absence was.

III.

It was the darkest night. It became the
brightest morning.
At least, it's the picture in my mind.
It was a long day. I walked and walked.
I had to stop to ask my way.

At dawn I came to you again and felt it was
time to put to rest ideas and dreams
of knowing you now, for my own need was
selfish. I had to let you go. You had to die and
I had to begin to live.

I was almost thirty.

IV.

We reached the hospital parking lot. It was
    enormous and empty back
in the corner where we danced.
Step, step, step.
I actually did not dance. I am not a dancer.
I marched because

I was at war, with living. With dying.
With forgetting. With remembering.

The sun was rising over a row of pine trees.
I was angry.
I marched to music I had never liked.
I began to circle.

Circle, circle, circle. The tides of life.

V.

In the back corner of the lot, I turned and
directly faced the rising sun—
I almost delighted in it.
Except, my work here was not delightful.
It was a tragedy.

I began to walk.
As I whistled my country march
the wind began to slowly stir and the dust on
the asphalt swirled around me.
I whistled louder, harder, stronger.
I inhaled deeply.
The wind responded.

I stopped.
I left you there.
I let you rest.

What Love Is

Just as I was preparing myself,
my home,
my harbor, my books,
For something really boring
in life,
You came whispering, barely speaking,
and you told me, you said,
"I'm right here."

Just as I began to wonder,
you kissed me.

And when I wondered again,
you held me for days,
And put a dream inside my ear.

You said,
"I know
the perfect

                place."

And just as I began to say something
to myself
about you,
You came calling, and you laid me down in a
quiet place,
and whispered,
and kissed me,
and we danced, and forgot about the moon,
only remembering,
as we danced,
when we were bathed in the dawn.

Cool Night Blue

Anne smoked a menthol cigarette in order
to engender the sensation of cold mornings,
of crispy Halloween air,
to torture herself with the memory:
of Mr. Cool #1, Mr. Ace of Spades,
who stole her heart right out
like he would a hubcap
or a chocolate bar,
And as she remembered the pain,
and the woe, and all that drama,
As she was remembering and driving home
from work crossing one side of town,
at 9:22 p.m., Mr. Cool #2, Mr. Blue,
Mr. Anne, was driving home from work
on the other side of town,
Same time. And as she remembered
the gravity of situation one,
she began to feel the enormity of situation
two, which is to say, Mr. Blue, he stuck
around, and his home was her home,
and there they lived together ever after.

So as Anne drove past Mr. Black's old house,
yep, he was back, and here as the past is now,
and he was sitting in front of the stolen TV,
and interrupting the life of
some sweet young—

while Anne was driving right on by him.
He was getting out of this car,
he was turning on that porch light:
He was in every home along the way all the
way to where boy Blue was out in his yard,
his porch light *on,* walking the dogs, and
waiting. And smiling as she passed the past,
quickly,
more quickly,
she began to embrace memories of meeting
the man in the band, the cool the blue,
the man who gave her his promise, and damn
he's still smiling & telling her he loves her
And when she says to him "he haunts me"
Mr. Cool #2 just quietly says
"I understand,"
like someone out there's been haunting
him too.

Winter

The bear hunts fish for the stomach
but I hunger for the food of thought.
I stand at the dam like a salmon
fixed on making my run. There
are so many people who want to take me
from the river, bareback— and tame me.
I say, "You cannot tame the bear.
You cannot tame these fish."

The dam floods and the hunters
enter the water.
I am the only one on watch,
waiting to see if the fish
will come around again,
as if they are my children.

You, Mr. Whitman

You, Mr. Whitman, became
in simple terms, a boy again—
& what mysteries you found there

came their way to me
through my living eyes:

while waving to us all,
you motioned and declared
You are the great among you!

Mr. Whitman— you're a spirit in the
strange, dark night,
catching me at these odd hours.

I stay awake in seek of treasures—and
sit among old men—
and discuss ideas & weather.

Before, I'd have guessed you are the Sun
who wakes me when the day's begun—

You bring on light with your lilting laughter
and bring an ease to my disaster.

But truly you are like the moon,
soothing me to sleep at night:

I'll forage and then drop away, off again
through tired eyes.

Mr. Whitman, how love is strange.
You tuck me into bed again.

I draw these words with a sleepy cadence—
my eyes take on the dew of night.

I'll walk with you beneath the moon,
and close my eyes— and close my eyes.

You softly sigh, &
softly, I.

The day, the day!
Your tears have washed the dew away.

Our Tree

I was a wild child
and I ran free
through the quiet streets of my little town.

I carried my dreams
in my feet,
running around my tree-sheltered streets.

Recently I went back around
to see the stone wall
I walked with bare feet—
my old cobblestone road,
my old street paved with gold.

I hardly recognized my street,
because the leg-up was gone
from my climbing tree.

Peace Vietnam: carved fervently:
in the low branch of my tree.

Somewhere someone else
will remember but me.

Eggshells

I spilled the glue
all over my hands
and then got stuck to the garbage
I was picking up after the dog.
Eggshells.

Now I'm sticking to this pen,
which has me sticking to you.

You are a true friend.

Tonight I felt like shouting,
walking and
looking up
at the sky,
noticing a full moon
for the first time all night.

It sticks to you, the moon.
It weaves its way
into your soul,
and touches
everything.

We are that moon.
We fill the sky.

Peace, Rhododendron

We swam before we walked,
"Like tadpoles," my mother says.
As children we walked barefoot
across our quiet street,
following no path,
through backyards down to the creek,
never thinking thoughts of trespassing.

Even on the coldest afternoons
we urged on the sun,
took off our shoes,
and walked the creek-bed picking up stones—
carrying between us a bucket of rocks.

It was in the cover of a rhododendron bush
that my sister and I sat
"cracking rocks"

pretending to be Friends.

I remember our times in chips & splinters:
the noise—
the silences—
the hard work—

        Always promising to pretend.

If we were not twins, perhaps
we never would have wanted so much
to be friends.
We would have missed
entangling our vines,
spilling and hoarding secrets at whim,
growing closer,
opening day by day,

us:

like stones, like sunshine, like friends.

If We Can Keep It

We left off at Trevi Fountain, Italia.
I gave you immortality of the gods,
and like a Queen of Hearts
I made pastries for the Knave to steal.

No one stole my tarts,
Now I'm giving you my heart:
Tell me two things about yourself,
now tell me two things about me.

It is beautiful to speak,
more beautiful in a new language; and
more beautiful, still
to let what is known
in the same alphabet
go unexplained—

More, unquestioned.

Ask me what love means
and I will teach you,
pointing down
through the days,

through tear-stained windows into

this
painting
of you.

We Called You Chief

I saw the sun setting in the desert
as slowly as it could wait for you.

Then night came 'round cold and angry
like a killer,

while

we all wished
to fill your day
with our alphabet of thoughts.

How tenderly your stoicism
touched us all
as you maneuvered life's great wheel,
walked the ladder—

                found your last clue—

The week began
with your beginning:

You traveled alone, without a ticket
as we watched from lonely sidewalks
silently in tears.

Exhausting All Media

I.

I worked in a warehouse
before dawn each day,
and missed knowing those days.

You were baking pizza in a shop at the beach,
starting your day as I was walking from the
bus stop back to my rented room.

I talked to spirits on the lawn
as I sat swinging, singing, dreaming—
my thoughts circling above me
quickly, like ducks.

Your shop survived a hurricane intact and
you lit up the ovens
and fed everybody.

I kicked out of the warehouse before
Halloween, heading east,
back home to an old job where
I would begin to feel real again.

II.

We both had known the thieves that
steal your heart like a hubcap;
each had kissed the jaded smiles of dragons;
and we both landed separately, on the cut-tin
edge of loneliness.

It was still years before I met you,
and before you met me.
I suppose we both preferred
our tin can sorrows
to hollow company.

More than fifteen years later, we would meet,
as if at the agreed-upon hour,
in a previously agreed-upon place,
beneath a dark sky, under a canopy of trees
that we jokingly conflated with a hobo's home
    (*galump galump!*).

III.

Now we sit here side by side, though busy
with our projects;
there is no jiving or news-making coming from
the television that stays off,
only the occasional sound
of a train across the street
and I look up when you say "freight,"
and we listen to the long, sad drone—and
when you smile

I feel like I am dancing in constellations
meeting you in the stars
for the very first time,
at a previously agreed-upon hour,
in a previously agreed-upon place,
strongly in your arms,
beneath a night that goes on forever.

Black Slush on the Roadside

Years later we were lost,
and stopped to eat burritos
in a small, strange town.
Then, as it began to snow,
it grew dark,
and when I woke up
from a small, strange nap,
it was all we could do
to find the old road.

We did, and
found a new supermarket,
four lanes, and
a prison
by your door out back.

You loved him because
you loved me.
And you cooked us breakfast
everyday at noon.

If you had said,
even whispered, "I'm leaving you,"
I could have held you knowing.

Daybreak

I think I would be okay,
I think I could make it out of bed each day—
if I had only to greet the sun,

to walk for berries to eat,
or to gather herbs, wildflowers, weeds—
tree-trunk bark and the nectar of bees.

It would become me to be
a woman of the past—
I resist technology,
I oppose progress.

I lie in my bed dreaming of peaceful days,
defying the certainty of Earth's careless decay.

Here

Here is a line in front of me
I am drawing in the sand.
I have been drawing it all my life.
Sometimes it looks like an "x."
Sometimes it is a cross.
Sometimes it is all I have;
At times it represents what I have lost.

One time I started to pull in my line
like I was fishing.
I made myself a pathway.
I dived into the sky.
I turned it into a black hole.
I made a moving sidewalk.

But someone put me in a cage,
by breaking into lines of rage
the line I held beside my heart.

So I made a love in the end of my line
that was a knot around my finger—

I give you my dreams.

I take you in and build a house.
You are quiet like a mouse.
You do not cross the line
between yours and mine:

"You go nowhere with me and
nowhere without me," you say.
I repeat. I do not know
what you say or what I say.

Only, you look at me, and
I don't feel like a ghost anymore,
and when I look back at the pain,
I am standing in the rain
and you are there,
and I have changed.

The Key of Light

I.

Monsters come from everywhere,
downstairs, from behind the darkness,
jumping out from hidden corners.

The antidote is tall
and tries
to make sense of it for me.

Memory takes me to my first glance
at your heroic face.

I seek now, and seek
to say what I have said,
because words are never adequate.

I am keener now
to celebrate all of the affections.

II.

Your ship was cruising
shallow waters, plough mud all around.
Sometimes I wonder how you remember it—

The island you wanted us to see,
the light in your eyes,
the joy in your spirit.

The hurrying tide began to erase safety:
And storms approached.

But happiness is contagious,
& we danced the boat beyond
the breaking waves,

and headed home.

We'll Feed the Animals

Passing stranger! you do not know how longingly I look upon you,
 You must be he I was seeking, or she I was seeking,

...You grew up with me, were a boy with me, or a girl with me,
 ...I am to wait—I do not doubt I am to meet you again,
 I am to see to it that I do not lose you.

— Walt Whitman, "To A Stranger," *Leaves of Grass*

Part One

I. Silhouette

When I was a child I loved you
and I believe, you loved me, too.
You showed up in corners of my day
around quiet neighborhoods
where I was running.

It has been impossible to explain
the numbers that I've played;
when, as a child, and as I grew:
you were me and I was you—
that in a way I cannot understand,
I have feared 'myself' — to love 'you.'

I did not know religion but that I wasn't
Presbyterian, Methodist, Episcopalienated,
and this I knew from looking up at you
while mysteries like love Divine
made a river of my deepest wishes.

There has always been this little girl,
a little child, an angel wild
Elziabeth and giant clouds—
with rain, and green, and everything

and wildest nights and wildflower days—
with just the hope
I'd know God's ways.

From penny dreams came red-light,
lazy river-ships of kindness given here.

II. Pentimento

You've been living by my side,
since the day we first came to.
Religion's Gap, gray pants & snaps—
new-born rap—and crap—
You dragged me through that foggy night,
Brother Blue—
to see in me, and see you— and me.

And kissed your head and tired not—
to behold in me, what I'd seen in you.

We were carried off our feet
through grass and country as we ran,
and in these fields and under moons,
we captured spells with starry eyes.
When we went down to the river there,
we sang and barked our heavenly ways,
that we'd give everything we had—
to just live in trees on quiet days.

I put you on a pedestal
and slammed and slammed
and locked the door
You told me of your garden wall,
where all your hidden secrets are:
and when I stayed away a while,
you brought me home—but let me fly;
and though your eyes are colorblind:
You kick my ass at Mastermind.

Meanwhile, hundred colors dance:
and meanwhile, knew you cared.

III. Opus, renewed

With a world-war menu change, which had us
rather watching channel 99,
than anything at all, and thus no longer
knowing what the 'e' in me or 'u' in you
in the world has to do with who I am,
I thought I died.

While from the back of the room
I came to wonder of your teaching:
to wander, wonder, think, and be: the world
I came to see, came from you and became me,
first, that you would take my face and name it:
a thousand times, and knowing, claim it—

Stopping now, and looking 'round,
Pacemaker Honey Bees, you gave my soul
to me: through games of heart—and TV stolen:
I was left here all alone
when you called me on the phone,
touched me gently,
& brought me home.

It's never too dark a night
when an angel comes
to bring back a name:

Soolaimon.

IV. *Laboring Through*

You awake me without doubt, and I arise,
a wiser Philadelphia babe:
An orphan boy, like, Jim, and him—
but not yet knowing, who *is* Jim?—
You packed my lunch, and I'm still feasting.
You wrote my books, and I'm still reading.
"Oh, no, Mr. Bill" my love is long,
You've made me beauty, full & strong.

V. *Travailler, chaque jour, chaque saime semaine*

Saime's not a word I know in French
but you'd have loved the funny trick,
I'm singing *Marseillaise* again:
and seek you here, and seek you there.
The chimes we hit on had no rules
We watched and laughed
and you, skilled: ruled. And you,
an actress, even better:

You wrote the funniest fucking letters.
The past is all that matters now.
Awesome, my love∼ Take your bow.

In glories and in thrills—to laugh—
could not be fair—
*I laugh—and you and I—and laugh—
and laugh—and laugh—and laugh.*

And without ticket, to the skies,
remember daily, you and I:

And having never said enough
but always, always, said too much!

So forgive me and I will you—
for all we actually *had to do*:
just smile, and calm, and down, and rise:
lift your head, and onward fly...

Part Two

I. The Contents of the Sea

There has always been a little angel child,
a girl like me, our nearby haven, with ghosts
that haunted—and long nights.

There were no clouds 'cause the clouds
were daisies, Ducks:
Strongly now, we've learned to be
"us" / "only."

If I could show you what you mean,
and give you raging, graceful dreams:
and give you what you've given me,
and tell you what you mean:
I'd have to start with the broken parts—
how I took a bit of your peacefulness:
while you'd explain the way we'd walk—
and you'd go that way, while I took off!

Little Shady Neighbor-Girl, I could tell you
things I've learned
from being two whole halves of "one"—
At times I hear us laughing now,
within our secret treehouse town.

Through lulls and drifting high above,
we give each other of this beauty.

II. *Walking Bridge*

Two mothers here, and gifted twice:
Friends with both, and with both fight:
Let me not begin to say the million words
I shouldn't say!

One reminds me, toasting "late"—
and blackest black,
and black off-scraping,
with "coming soon," and "I'll be back."
Hours pass and you are slowly
helping see me through my learning.

When I ask what you'll be doing,
and knocking twice say: *listening for you*—
You'll cock your head, slowly now, to the back,
and smile, which has become your laugh:

You say, just, *have me see again:*
I want to see the words again,
and sing again, and sing like you:
And nightly off to sleeping drift,
and don't you worry: only "keep."

III. *What Love's Like*

We found religion but we've always had song,
and having run, you brought me Home.
And made me Keeper of the Gate:
with silent, goodnight, starry touch:
and placed your heart beneath my head,
and drifted me away to bed.

While you are sleeping I am fine:
and kick on over, every time—
it's not a lot of time we share,
except it all: and that seems "fair."

* * *

Young Tom Thumb was never that,
and "Bulbs" & such, and "Molly Mac"—
some things I rhyme you did not know:
and here you'll say, "Whelp! There she goes!!"

Alrighty light you're a window light:
Without you I don't function right.

But I am sleeping 'til I wake,
and dreaming, dream of keeping dates
of redneck love, which will not wait.

* * *

Cliff-Height View: it was me & you
I "never knew"—from here—
the view, from here: the view—
from here: the view.

You took the hyphens out of me,
and took away my misery:
indulged me in some mystery—
and taught me explosive chemistry.

You put *real* silver in my smile:
And walked with me a thousand miles.

We built a window to the Sun: and off we sing,
    and away we run.

—It's time here, soon, for Labor Day
and late at night, perhaps we'll play—

While your song shines
to my heart's reveling...
& music box paintings & windows & flying.

"We have love's love like piano whispers"
you quietly say,

We have love's love
because we have loved

           —love's forte.

Acknowledgments

In addition to being my hero and my best friend, my twin sister, Mary-Margaret, kept a collection of my poems for more than twenty years before handing it back to me without storage fees. That collection is part of what you have in your hands, and revisiting it with MM's encouragement sparked my recent efforts.

James D. McCallister is a brilliant writer and thinker, very gently patient, and truly my co-creator on this project. In addition to his beautiful reflections, wisdom, thoughtful 'assignments,' and enthusiasm (all of which have genuinely lifted me up), the details of this project are his. My friend, my mentor, my Dropbox penpal, Dmac has cared about these poems and found light in them; and that makes his involvement an exponential honor.

My father, Steve Leverton, has been a constant supporter of my development as an individual and as an artist. My dad is a giver, a thoughtful man, a quiet warrior, and a lover of the arts: and I adore him.

Stephanie Alise has encouraged my love for creativity, and always plans big. Susana Berdecio's thoughtful feedback pushes me to create thoughtfully. William Christopher shows great enthusiasm in encouraging this path I'm on. Debbie Clark's joy is contagious, and her gentle guidance changes me. Cathy Cobbs took an immediate interest in my art and has contributed to my continuing it. Amanda Dalola has ignited my self-esteem by staying up night-owl late with me and scientifically explaining to me that it's okay to have too much fun. Sharon Davis has inspired me to be more like her, courageous and loving. Sarah Efird has inspired me to fly, through her example of turning expert flips in the air. Karen and David Fechter have been family to me since I met them. Britt Ferro's grace and humor is tangibly amazing and millions-billions inspiring, in friendship and in art. Carrie Finch has shared a beautiful sense of humor that reminds me not to take myself too seriously. If not for Kathy Flanagan's love and forgiveness, I would not be where I am today. Patricia Flanagan offers kind encouragement that moves me to turn my dreams into art. Fly is the godfather of decency, inspiring me in ways he does not imagine. Hillary Greason and Mike Dunn are family who always bring me home. May Evans Kirby has listened to me read poetry over coffee and has steadfastly believed in me. David Kurtz has been, in that rare way, a forever friend (however distant). Katherine Lang was an early reader who suggested I share my poems years ago. My nephew Stephen checks in with me and is infinitely inspiring. Jenn McCallister insisted that I sing my song when she could have done it better. Jennifer Lee and Chris McCormick have filled in so many holes by being cheerful and loving—and are always enthusiastic about my art. Amy Catherine McCormick, who we lost to cancer, was a major comfort, advisor, mentor, sister-friend, and inspiration in my life. My "spiritual twin," Marybeth McDonnell, is an enthusiastic co-conspirator in troubleshooting life & creating art. Jamie and Fred Mansperger are dear friends who graciously read early versions of some of these poems. Valerie Martin has always inspired me to believe in peace. The Meyer-Gutbrod family brings immense amounts of joy into my creative space. So do my Park nieces, who never shy away from markers and blank paper when I'm around. Eliza Park told me when she was eight that I could do anything, and I'm trying not to disappoint her. My sister Sarah Perdue has shown up for me when it counted most. Maura Rieman is a lifeline for me, who has suggested for years that I collect my notes into a book. Karri Scollon consistently encourages me to honor my imagination. Gretchen Segars has been my *simpatico* since the moment we met each other, and she has been deeply encouraging of my efforts in creativity. Art Shoemaker is a light whose smiles break through the darkest clouds. Becky Siceloff quietly inspires me in radical ways. Whitney Waites is a compassionate friend who always notices where I am. James Walker gives meaningful feedback in gentle ways. I find his ideas to be incredibly inventive and refreshing, and I happily consider him to be my overarching creative director.

    Tom Mayne helped me begin again with his continuing patience, compassion, and bright ideas. Betsy McWhite showed deep kindness and provided assistance that helped me go for it.

    Ken Williams has shown kind enthusiasm over my art—and he and the rest of our team tolerate an artsy personality in the workplace with good humor.

    Frances Young and Jay Croft at Midlands Technical College shined up my dull skillset along with my smile.

    My friend and art teacher, Alicia Leeke, always believes I can do better. I mean, that's a little annoying, but ultimately inspiring.

    My mother, Betty, has a heart of gold & maintains enthusiasm about my art no matter how offbeat it is.

Beyond the valuable encouragement they've shown regarding my art and writing, my brother, Bill Leverton, and his wife, Taryn, saved my life when it was not easy to do so.

My high-school Civics teacher, David Morris, has inspired me for more than thirty years. David was my long-term penpal when I was at an age of big questions. We passed thoughts about books and ideas back and forth for more than ten years—and David has never seen me since without asking if I am still writing. His wife, Kelley, supported my art early on by encouraging me to develop my own direction freely.

My high-school English teacher, Becky Costner, believed in me when I didn't realize how much it would positively affect my life. She was extremely cheerful and gave me the space and support to learn in my own way.

Six people at Eckerd College instilled passion in my approach to learning: my mentor, Claire Stiles, who opened up the sky and made thought and creativity a delight; Molly Ransbury (who encouraged my writing); my drawing professor, Margaret Rigg, who believed I had it in me; and Sterling Watson (whose brilliant writing workshop sparked something in my heart). My friends Michele Whaling (my roommate who joined me in rigorous study and in travels) and Monique Rice made the Florida rain not matter.

Bruce Kawin at The University of Colorado-Boulder created a Modern Poetry class that spanned from Sappho to contemporary poetry. The reading list, which included two collections he expertly curated for the class, was brilliant, comprehensive, and overwhelming. The immersion into this art form that Bruce provided taught me above all to love poetry rather than fear it.

Tony Hoagland at Warren Wilson's ten-day writing residency believed in my positive intentions and encouraged me to continue writing.

I learned so much about writing working under Richard Layman at Bruccoli Clark Layman.

I've also learned a lot about writing working under Barry Stanton, who has always treated me like a colleague, and whose writing is absolutely beautiful.

About the Author

Elizabeth Leverton earned a BA in English Lit and a master's degree in English with a concentration in writing and editing at The University of North Carolina at Greensboro. She began writing poetry thirty years ago. A recent graduate of the Commercial Graphics program at Midlands Technical College, Elizabeth is a graphic designer/typesetter who also enjoys songwriting and playing guitar, singing karaoke, dancing, swimming, tennis, sewing functional art, and acrylic painting. She lives in Columbia, South Carolina, with her Labrador Retriever, Molly, and part-Siamese sister cats, Silo and Weaver. *Peace, Rhododendron* is her first book.

Also Available From

King's Highway
Fellow Traveler
Let the Glory Pass Away
The Year They Canceled Christmas
Dogs of Parsons Hollow
Dixiana
Down in Dixiana
Dixiana Darling
Mansion of High Ghosts
Reconstruction of the Fables
By
James D. McCallister

Feint
Sailing Off the Edge of the World
By
Michael G. Sullivan

Dream Work
By
R. Bentz Kirby

CPSIA information can be obtained
at www.ICGtesting.com
Printed in the USA
LVHW041941080723
751854LV00004B/81

9 781946 052476